A Lenten
African Am

ON MA JOURNEY NOW

Gwendolyn Brown-Felder

STUDENT

Abingdon Press / Nashville

ON MA JOURNEY NOW:
A LENTEN STUDY BASED ON AFRICAN AMERICAN SPIRITUALS
STUDENT BOOK

Copyright © 2005 by Abingdon Press

All rights reserved.

Scripture quotations in this publication, unless otherwise indicated, are from the New Revised Standard Version of the Bible, copyright © 1989 by the Division of Christian Education of the National Council of the Churches of Christ in the United States of America, and are used by permission.

Slave quotations are taken from the public records of the Library of Congress.

Electronic text from the Web site http://docsouth.unc.edu is property of the University of North Carolina at Chapel Hill.

This book is printed on acid-free, elemental chlorine-free paper.

ISBN 0-687-05342-0

Lead Editor: Marilyn E. Thornton

05 06 07 08 09 10 11 12 13 14 —10 9 8 7 6 5 4 3 2 1

MANUFACTURED IN THE UNITED STATES OF AMERICA

Contents

"I sho is glad I ain't no slave no moah. Ah thank God that ah lived to pas the yeahs [years] until the day of 1937. Ah'm happy and satisfied now, and ah hopes to see a million yeahs to come."
(Richard Toler, former slave, Lynchburg, VA, 1937)

Introduction

On *Ma Journey Now: A Lenten Study Based on African American Spirituals* is the sixth in a series of Bible studies that utilize both Scripture and song to interpret God's movement in our lives and in the world. The first in the series is *Plenty Good Room* (2002), followed by the Advent study *Mary Had a Baby* (2003), then *Ride On, Jesus* (2004), *Come Out de Wilderness* (spring 2005), and most recently *Don't Let This Harvest Pass* (summer 2005), which is based on spirituals that focus attention on giving thanks and the season of Thanksgiving. The entire series uses the African American spiritual as a way of centering the perspective, culture, history, and needs of the African American community in the study of the Bible. Three of the studies also focus on crucial Christian seasons and celebrations. *On Ma Journey Now* is one of these.

On Ma Journey Now is designed to assist you as you prepare your spirit during the Lenten season for the observance of the Easter celebration. It is traditional for persons practicing Lent also to practice a fast of some kind, giving up a favorite food and/or abstaining from some kind of activity that is creating a barrier to spiritual growth. Lent begins with Ash Wednesday, in which persons in many denominations place ashes on their foreheads. The ashes are the burnt remnants of the previous year's palms, the palms of Palm Sunday, with which people greeted Jesus as King only to have him murdered by Friday. During the Lenten season, we journey through the passion of Christ as he suffers and dies. Fasting, ashes, and crying aloud are rituals of repentance and mourning as practiced in the Old Testament (Esther 4:1; Daniel 9:3). We participate in these ancient rituals during Lent.

In *On Ma Journey Now*, we cry aloud in song through the African American spiritual. Most of the spirituals used in this study are "sorrow songs," a genre uniquely appropriate for drawing us into a period of mourning for our own sins as well as for the sins of the world. Coming from the souls of African American slaves, these songs lift up their strengths and concerns, illuminating the religion that held them together and kept them moving forward. Sorrow songs also naturally lead us to reflect upon the sins of slavery and racism and all the accompanying ills. We invite you to moan and mourn with those who were enslaved.

We invite you to travel with Jesus as he shows us how to resist the evils of the world. With this study, we hope that you will gather strength for the journey of life.

Marilyn E. Thornton,
Lead Editor

Session 1

This Lonesome Valley

Matthew 4:1-4

Key Verse: But he [Jesus] answered, "It is written, 'One does not live by bread alone, / but by every word that comes from the mouth of God'" (Matthew 4:4).

Opening Prayer: O God, you are our comfort. You come to us when we are lonely and depressed. Help us see the needs of others and share your comfort with them. Amen.

Spiritual: Jesus Walked This Lonesome Valley

"Jesus Walked This Lonesome Valley"

Chorus:
Jesus walked this lonesome valley.
He had to walk it by himself.
Oh, nobody else could walk it for him.
He had to walk it by himself.

I must walk this lonesome valley.
We must walk this lonesome valley.

Let's Listen: A Song of Freedom

While spirituals can show us that some were motherless and fatherless and longed for a place to call home, "Jesus Walked This Lonesome Valley" reveals the loneliness of many in the enslaved community. With this spiritual, Christian slaves could experience God's empathy. It describes a God who affirmed their humanity and related to their situation. Jesus' experience of a lonely journey of suffering and sacrifice was a day-to-day occurrence for many slaves. They could relate to a lonesome valley experience. Indeed, this song offered encouragement to those enslaved in a brutal system of oppression.

Sung meaningfully at a walking tempo, these simple lyrics brought to life the slaves' deeply rooted feelings of solitude. This sacred song was used as a means of inspiration. They knew that if Jesus could make it through the valley, with his strength they could too. Whether sung in their most discouraging moments or while wading the waters to freedom, the slaves were inspired to believe that Jesus would help them.

In his book *The Spirituals and the Blues,* theologian James H. Cone explains, "The 'I' of black slave religion was born in the context of the brokenness of black existence. It was an affirmation of self in a situation where the decision to *be* was thrust upon the slaves…. The 'I,' then, who cries out in the spirituals is a particular black self affirming both his or her being and being-in-community, for the two are inseparable."[1] Additionally, Jesus promised, "I am with you always, to the end of the age" (Matthew 28:20b). We are never alone; God is with us. Even though humanity or individuals withdraw themselves from us and are not available, God is present. God is there in our lonesome valleys and in our happy hilltops. Hence the singer sings with determination, "We must walk…."

The Middle Passage

There was no lonelier valley than that of the Middle Passage, the transport of black Africans to the Americas by slave ship. Nowhere in the records of history have a people experienced such a long and indescribably traumatic ordeal as Africans during the trans-Atlantic slave trade. For a period of almost four centuries, millions of Africans began the voyage in which it is estimated that only one third survived. The Middle Passage was so called because it was the middle leg of a three-part voyage that began and ended in Europe. The first leg of the voyage carried cargo that often included iron, cloth, brandy, firearms, and gunpowder. Upon landing on Africa's western coast, the cargo was exchanged for Africans, who were often victims of war and greedy tribal leaders. Those captured often walked hundreds of miles, herded from their homes to reach coastal forts where they might wait as long as a year for departure. After loading their emptied cargo holds with captured Africans, the middle leg of the journey began. Upon reaching the Americas, the Africans were sold as slaves, and the traders in turn purchased raw sugar, tobacco, and cotton for the return trip—the third leg—to Europe.

The Middle Passage was a most horrific journey. Ships traveled west across the Atlantic on trips lasting from five weeks to a year. Most Africans who survived did not return to the homeland to tell their story. Conditions aboard the ships were deadly. Three to four hundred people were shackled, packed like sardines between decks in tiny areas. Ventilation was poor. They lay in common beds of bodily wastes. Disease often broke out, and those infected were tossed overboard like trash. Faced with such conditions and an unknown future, many Africans preferred death. Some tried to starve themselves by refusing to eat. Others tried jumping overboard. However, slaves who would not eat were whipped and/or force-fed. Then, the ship's crews began fixing nets to the sides of the boat so that the slaves could not jump overboard, leaving no choice but to endure the horrible conditions.

The Africans were from different tribes and communities; therefore, they were unable to communicate the pain of suffering, grief of loss, and the fears of the unknown to comfort one another. Only groans and tears could express their sorrow and pain. They were lonely and alone. No one could walk this lonesome valley for them. No one could travel this wilderness experience for them. A new place with new customs and new languages caused much fear and desperation for the Africans. What a lonely feeling! How could one survive such a tragedy?

It is good to know that the Africans who survived had a God who eased their fears and soothed their pain as they traveled the lonesome valley. The terrible Middle Passage and America's slave institution have come to represent a virtual wilderness in human misery and suffering, a lonesome valley indeed.[2]

The Wilderness: Matthew 4:1-3

Peoples and individuals throughout history have endured lonesome valley and wilderness experiences. Why does God lead us into the wilderness? Could it be a preparation before great trials or testing for a great work? Having empowered Jesus for his mission as God's Son (Matthew 3:16-17), the Spirit leads him into the wilderness, where his calling must be tested. Jesus provides a model for believers who go through a time of tests. Jesus is our champion who fights on behalf of all people. Christians are destined for testing (Matthew 6:13; 26:41); but Jesus, our forerunner, has shown us how to overcome.

Jesus' time in the wilderness parallels that of the Hebrew people in Exodus and Numbers. The desert or the wilderness is not a pleasant place. The Hebrew word for wilderness is *midbar,* which means "without word." The wilderness is a place that is desolate of human words. Struggle, solitude, and sacrifice are familiar elements in the wilderness. However, it is often a place where the Word of God resonates. The wilderness can be a place of prayer. There, we seek God's direction, guidance, strength, and wisdom and ask for better ways to live together.

Time is a factor in the wilderness, and the number forty is significant. The Hebrew children wandered in the wilderness for forty years. Jesus fasted and dwelled in the wilderness for forty days and nights. The period of Lent is forty days long, not including Sundays. For the slaves, days turned into weeks, weeks into months, months into years, and years into centuries. Suffering is bad enough, lonesomeness troubling, but to endure these hardships for what seems to be an eternity is devastating.

When God is calling and empowering you to do something, you can expect tests. You can expect a testing relative to the seriousness of your calling. The devil may not show up in person or test you on the same supernatural level that he attempted to test Jesus, but your troubles may still seem unbearable, apart from the grace of God. Nevertheless, testing is for our good, even if we do not know all the reasons for the testing. The Hebrew children had to endure testing in the wilderness in order to gain a national identity and to learn the ways of God. Jesus had to pass a period of testing before beginning his public ministry. There are those who believe that black people had to endure slavery in order to become Christians. This idea leaves at least three questions unanswered: Why then did not all of the enslaved become Christian, why was it necessary for the enslavers to teach a racist brand of Christianity, and did not God have the power to bring Christianity to Africans in Africa (Acts 8:26-38)? Regardless of the whys and wherefores, Jesus provides the perfect model for passing tests and overcoming trials.

> *"If we had money we had to tu'n it ovah to ouah ownah. Chu'ch was not allowed in ouah pa't neithath. Ah go to the Meth'dist Chu'ch now, everybody ought to go. I think RELIGION MUST BE FINE, 'CAUSE GOD ALMIGHTY'S AT THE HEAD OF IT."*
> *(Richard Toler, former slave, Lynchburg, VA, 1937)*

The First Test: Matthew 4:4

The devil tests Jesus with three situations. In the Book of Job, the devil is called Satan (*ha-satan*), Hebrew for "the accuser." It is the devil's job to oppose, accuse, and stand against the faithful. The first test was about definition. What was the Son of God's role—magician or Messiah? The devil tries to tempt Jesus to abuse his calling and power for selfish ends. God identifies Jesus as his Son (Matthew 3:16-17); now the devil tries to redefine the nature of Jesus as the Son of God. His challenge "if you are the Son of God" (4:3) can also be translated "since you are the Son of God," which may be more likely in this context. Jesus had been fasting for forty days and nights. Simply, Satan tells Jesus, "Since you are God's son, you can do magic. You can turn these stones into bread. Do it!"

Fortunately, Jesus is not a magician but the Messiah, the one anointed to accomplish God's salvation. Magicians typically sought to transform one substance into another to demonstrate their power. Jesus did not have to demonstrate his power. He knew who he was and whose he was. He was not trying to impress anyone or gain support. All through Jesus' ministry, he had opponents who could not deny his power but wished to attribute it to Satan, as if he were a magician or sorcerer (Matthew 12:24). And though he had the power to multiply food (Matthew 14:13-21; 15:32-38), he resisted the temptation to turn stones into bread. Jesus refused to be defined by worldly rules, resisted the devil, and admonished him with the Word: "It is written, 'One does not live by bread alone, / but by every word that comes from the mouth of God'" (4:4). The devil invites Jesus not so much to deny being the Son of God but rather to adapt to worldly expectations for that role. This Scripture lesson warns all of us not to let the world define the content of our calling.

John Wesley is a good example of one who defined his own ministry. Contrary to the practices of the Anglican Church, of which he was a priest, John Wesley claimed the world as his parish. Wesley went into other parishes to reach people who were not being served: the poor, uneducated, and alienated. His calling did not fit the Anglican definition, yet he began a holiness revival with music and practices that can be found among Methodist, Baptist, Pentecostal, Holiness, Wesleyan, and Nazarene denominations. We, like Wesley—and ultimately like Jesus—must conduct our ministries according to the definitions of a God who calls us.

Ponder and Wonder: Wilderness Experience

How is God present in places where there seems to be no Word? Is God present in any wilderness experience, be it Israel's exodus, the Middle Passage, the European Holocaust, or our own personal struggle? The answer is that we are never alone. Just as the presence of God was with the Hebrew children in a pillar of fire and smoke (Exodus 13:21-22), God's grace and presence surround us. Jesus was not alone in the wilderness; he had and we have the ever-pervasive presence of the Holy Spirit. God was with Jesus, God was with those in the bottom of the slave ships, and God is with us now.

A wilderness experience makes us strong. We fast during Lent for spiritual empowerment. Jesus' being sanctified leads to our sanctification. The Holy Spirit led Jesus into the wilderness and sustained him in the midst of temptation. All temptation comes from Satan, who uses our friends, our enemies, and even our own minds. By faith, we can meet the challenges of temptation. Like Jesus, our faith is strengthened through the written and spoken Word of God. This Lenten season, let us draw closer to God individually and as a community. Each person has lonesome valleys, but through Jesus Christ and with the people of God, we can be strengthened for faithful living.

Food for Thought

1. What do you believe enabled the captured Africans to cope with their lonesome valley experience?
2. How do you handle times when you feel like you are alone in a situation?
3. What does a wilderness experience mean to you?
4. How do you define your ministry?
5. What are your goals for this Lenten season?

Closing Prayer

Gracious God, you have blessed us to live in community, never to be alone. Help us always to recognize that we should help and support each other. Amen.

Session 2

A City Called Heaven

Matthew 4:5-7

> **Key Verse:** Jesus said to him, "Again it is written, 'Do not put the Lord your God to the test'" (Matthew 4:7).
>
> **Opening Prayer:** Dear God, Creator of heaven and earth, in you we find hope. Teach us to follow you more closely so that we may bring hope to others. Amen.
>
> **Spiritual:** A City Called Heaven

"A City Called Heaven"

I am a poor pilgrim of sorrow.
I'm tossed in this wide world alone.
No hope have I for the morrow.
I'm tryin' to make heaven my home.
Sometimes I am tossed and driven, Lord.
Sometimes I don't know where to roam.
I've heard of a city called heaven.
I've started to make heaven my home.

Let's Listen: A Song of Despair and Hope

"A City Called Heaven" is a song of despair, a sorrow song that begins with a mournful moan. It is sung slowly with expression, the message and cry for relief ringing clear. The song features a poor pilgrim of sorrow—a wanderer, a person who travels about without a place to call home. The pilgrim has endured much grief, and this weary soul needs to find rest. She has heard of a city called heaven and is resolved to make heaven her home. One can see how such lyrics sprang from the souls of enslaved Africans, wandering far from their villages across a vast body of water to a place where people with white skins dominated them. This pilgrimage feels hopeless. There appears to be no hope on earth, so the pilgrim chooses to make heaven her home, where spiritual and physical freedom abounds.

"A City Called Heaven" is a song of hope. The wonderful flexibility of this song allows for several meanings: Heaven is the internal spirit, here and now. Heaven is the land of freedom, in the North. Heaven is a home in Mother Africa. Heaven is also life after death in a place more hospitable than the one in which they roamed, tossed from plantation to plantation, separated from family, and driven by overseers as beasts of burden. The connection or anticipation of any or all of these dimensions of heaven helps the singer to persevere, struggle, resist, and maintain a solid sense of self as a child of God.

The melody assists the lyrics in depicting the despair of the slave on the plantation as well as reflecting the hope for a city called heaven. The opening words are sung between two notes, using the interval of a minor third. This musical interval is characteristic of sadness in the blues and in European song. As the song describes the plight of its creators, the melody alternates between the two notes like a tossed and driven soul, dipping down into the depths on the word *alone*. Yet on *heaven* there is a lift—a lift in spirit as indicated by a higher note—followed by a resolute statement of purpose: to make heaven home. The African American slave had no home but heaven.

Pilgrims of Sorrow

Records indicate that in 1619, twenty Africans were brought to Jamestown as indentured servants. During early colonial times, black servants had the same rights as white servants, receiving housing and food in exchange for free labor. Indentured servants were contracted to work for a certain length of time to pay off a debt or passage from afar. Blacks were not at first considered servants for life. Those who broke their contracts were punished in the same manner, whether black or white. At the end of their term, they received "freedom dues," often including property, supplies, and a gun.

Anthony Johnson was a free black man who owned property in Virginia. He was brought to the colony in 1621. The 1625 Virginia census refers to him as "Antonio the Negro." It calls him a servant, not a slave. At this time, English and Colonial law did not define racial slavery. However, this was only temporary. With gradual speed, a race-based slave system was established by law, justified by ideology, and maintained by violence. Justification for the enslavement of black people rested on three suppositions attributed to the Africans: 1) They were cursed as descendants of Ham, marked with black skin and doomed to wander (Genesis 9:25-27). 2) They were savages; Africans did not have English cultural refinement. 3) Africans were pagan and non-Christian. With this ideology and desire for free labor, the whites created a new social and economic system. By 1662, the colony of Virginia created laws that imposed slavery on all children born to a slave mother. Slavery became a life-long condition that was passed on—like skin color—from generation to generation. Enforced servitude was gradually established in America, one law at a time, one colony at a time. By 1710, Africans began to out-number Europeans in many southern colonies. With free, cheap, and permanent workers available to harvest rice, tobacco, and cotton, plantation owners began to amass great wealth, and a once-free people became pilgrims of sorrow.[3]

Heard of a City

Although enslaved and characterized as inferior, many Africans found hope in the midst of a hopeless situation. They heard of a city called heaven and recognized the dwelling place of the Supreme Being they had always known. They found a friend in a Jesus whose teachings were markedly different from what the slave masters practiced in the name of Jesus. Some may have accepted Christianity due to the social freedoms allowed to them through Sunday worship and Christian celebrations. Christianity eased the cultural shock many Africans experienced and allowed them social development. While the drum was

> *"The slaves used to dance or go to prayer meeting to pass their time.... There was always a big celebration on Christmas. We worked until Christmas Eve and from that time until New Year's we had a vacation." (Clayton Holbert, former slave in Tennessee, 1937)*

outlawed, the communal singing and storytelling of camp meetings were reminiscent of African practices. Secret prayer meetings served to foster a sense of hope among the slaves. Promises of a better afterlife encouraged the oppressed slaves to look for something better, beyond what they received in reality.

Christianity sustained hope in a community even as it created a paradox. How could the slave masters "praise God on Sunday and then beat a slave near death on Monday"? Such hypocrisy, no doubt, kept many slaves from believing. Frederick Douglass was a runaway slave and an orator for freedom who became a member of the AMEZ church. He made this and many comments on the differences between the Christianity of Christ and that of America: "I love the pure, peaceable, and impartial Christianity of Christ: I therefore hate the corrupt, slaveholding, women-whipping, cradle-plundering, partial and hypocritical Christianity of this land."[4] Ultimately, Christianity was the driving motivator for antislavery activists. Many pamphlets and speeches made the case for the immorality of slavery, arguing that only God has ownership of human beings. Though slavery in America is gone, the racism that it spawned is still present. During this Lenten season, let us pray and seek ways to eliminate racism. Surely its end will give us a taste of heaven.

The Second Test: Matthew 4:5-7

With this second test, the devil takes Jesus to Jerusalem and places him on the highest tower of the temple. Then he dares Jesus to jump. "Nothing is going to happen to you, Jesus. You're so important that the angels of God will save you. You won't even stub a toe. That's what it says in the Bible!!" Jesus was committed to obedience to God's will, not his own (Mark 14:36). Satan's suggestion that Jesus jump from the top of the temple was presumptuous. The devil wanted Jesus to act without God's guidance. God had not told Jesus to jump. His loyalty was to the Father, not to Satan. For Jesus to jump and God to save him would mean God was there to serve the Son rather than the Son there to serve the Father.

When we become so wise as to think we have God figured out, we can easily miss God's true purpose and become Satan's worker. We must decide for whom we are working. Those who misquoted and misinterpreted the words of a God of freedom to establish oppression allowed themselves to be workers of the devil. We must be careful how we use God's Word, never failing to worship God in spirit and in truth as we study and share.

The Holy Spirit, not Satan, led Jesus into the wilderness. He had no claim for Satan's cause. When we find ourselves venturing ahead with our personal agendas, acting out of our own desires without prayer and the Spirit, we will encounter some uncomfortable surprises. The lesson for the Christian is to be sensitive to the Spirit's lead and to do what God calls us to do. It is not for us to put God to the test or lead and guide God. We are the children of God in service. When God has genuinely spoken, his servants act in obedience, and God accomplishes the purpose.

It was not Jesus' purpose to test God. He warned Satan against putting God to the test (Matthew 4:7), because Jesus knew the consequences of such behavior. The children of Israel had wandered in the wilderness for forty years because of their disobedience. Although God graciously supplied their needs, they not only tested God's patience by demanding more, they actually worshiped a golden calf and forgot how God had delivered them.

Like Jesus, we too are tested. People aiming to get your last dollar by daring you to demand a blessing from God tell you to jump. "Dare God to get you that luxury car!" The fact of the matter is that a generous God has already supplied our needs. We must dedicate our substance to God in order to use it rightly. Surely America could have been built without slave labor, perhaps not as quickly, perhaps with the wealth more evenly distributed, perhaps even with more freedom and justice for all. We dare God and expect God to save us. However, just as slavery has reaped a crop of continuing woes for America, demands that test God will have evil rewards. As we move through this Lenten season, let us examine and repent of the ways in which we dare God.

Ponder and Wonder: Resisting Temptation

Resisting temptation is not an easy task. Resisting a dare carries the risk of being called "Chicken!" It may mean being out of step with the mainstream culture. Many times we are tempted and drawn away by our own lust, by life's disappointments, or by materialistic agendas. The famous question "What would Jesus do?" (WWJD) can be used as a guide in our time of testing. There were whites who resisted being part of the mainstream culture that permitted slavery. They looked to the Scriptures in which Jesus said that he came to "proclaim release to the captives / and…let the oppressed go free" (Luke 4:18). Jesus chose to resist the evil and temptation of the riches that slavery could bring. Scripture informs us that Jesus responded to each of the devil's tests with the Word. Jesus, the Word in flesh, came as man to experience life so that we may understand and have an example to follow. Sometimes our culture is enough to cause us to throw up our hands and give in, but we can decide to have a hope in heaven by adhering to heavenly values. As we labor in earthly cities where Satan tempts and tests us, let us strive to make our homes more heavenly.

Food for Thought

1. What was going on in the life of the slave community to inspire the lyrics to the song?
2. Think about your last experience with temptation. Did God provide a way of escape? If so, did you take it?
3. How would you explain to youth or teenagers ways of dealing with tempting moments in their lives?

Closing Prayer

Oh gracious God, our strength in times of weakness, remembering our failures is bitter to us. Help us to depend on you for our help and to help others in their time of temptation. For Christ's sake we pray. Amen.

Session 3

Bow Down on Your Knees

Matthew 4:8-11

Key Verse: Jesus said to him, "Away with you, Satan!
for it is written, 'Worship the Lord your God
/ and serve only him'" (Matthew 4:10).

Opening Prayer: Dear Jesus, our Redeemer and Lord, in you
we find shelter. Help us always to know that
we have a home in you, a special place
prepared for us.

Spiritual: Po' Mou'ner's Got a Home at Last

"Po' Mou'ner's Got a Home at Last"

Refrain:
No harm, no harm, go tell Brother Elijah,
No harm, no harm, po' mou'ner's got a home at last.

Verse 1:
Mou'ner, mou'ner, ain't you tired o' mou'nin'?
Bow down on your knees and pray.
Mou'ner, mou'ner, ain't you tired o' mou'nin'?
J'ine (join) de band with the angels.

Verse 2:
Sinner, sinner, ain't you tired o' sinnin'?

Verse 3:
Gambler, gambler, ain't you tired o' gamblin'?

Let's Listen: Blessing Those Who Mourn

"Po' Mou'ner's Got a Home at Last" is a sorrow song with at least two goals: One is to call the sinner to repentance. The other is assurance that "those who mourn…will be comforted" (Matthew 5:4). The slaves lived in harsh circumstances. They could be sold, killed while trying to escape, or die working in the fields or from punishment. The refrain of this song declares that there is no harm to the believer in whatever happens, for as Paul says, "Living is Christ and dying is gain" (Philippians 1:21).

The lyrics of the refrain call on Elijah the prophet. The slave community often used Old Testament characters to tell their stories. Because many African cultures maintained an active connection with ancestors, it is easy to see this natural connection with biblical brothers and sisters. Although they were bound in shackles on the outside, worship would set them free on the inside. They found an intimate contact with God and their heavenly friends. Jesus and the Old Testament characters were presented as friends, family members who helped them through their struggles.

Sung slowly and prayerfully, these lyrics expressed the slaves' compassion and love for one another. They did not want to see each another in pain and suffering. This song is a plea for those who seem to be unaware of the rewards of worship. The melody and rhythm accommodate the lyrics in persuading the non-Christian and Christian slave to bow down to the God of salvation. The verses give a heartrending plea to mourners, sinners, and gamblers to give up their current activities and join the angel band. They speak to us during this Lenten season to set aside daily activities—sinful and otherwise—to join in the worship and study of God.

Po' Mou'ner's Got a Home

It must have been reassuring to know that no matter how dire the circumstances, those who went about mournfully would find a home. Home is a place where the soul and the body are nurtured. Making a home, finding accommodations, and keeping their families healthy and intact were major challenges for the slave community. How can you make a place of peace and comfort in slavery? On some plantations, workers received only leftover pot likker and bread. Meat was a delicacy reserved for Christian celebration times. Molasses and bread was a standard meal for the slaves; these two ingredients gave the slaves energy for working. Some plantation owners were generous and rationed out a peck of cornmeal and two to four pounds of bacon (salt pork) a week to each full hand.

Home-places were meager one- or two-room cabins. Some slaves were required to sleep at the foot of the bed of the master's children and not allowed to sleep with their own family, which is the most important ingredient for a home. Blacks were not considered fully human and were not expected to maintain a family unit. They were considered as above-average animals. There is no doubt that slavery injured black family life and left scars that damage black Americans to the present time. Mothers, fathers, and children were sold away from one another, making it difficult to maintain a family. It

> *"I don't know where I been born. Nobody never did tell me. But my mammy and pappy git me after de War and I know den whose child I is." (Lucinda Davis, former slave of Creek Indians, Oklahoma, 1937)*

cannot be denied that the slave family took a tremendous beating; its members were sold to satisfy creditors and purchased to increase personal wealth. It was most difficult for the slave to make a home out of this hopeless situation.

So, how did the slaves find a new home, community, accommodations, and acceptance? Whether white-led or in the hush arbors of the invisible church, they found a new home in Christ. Their Christian belief brought them acceptance into the community of faith. In many black churches even now, persons are called brother and sister, indicating a spiritual kinship. This practice no doubt began in slavery. No matter how distant family ties became, many slaves adjusted through the church and extended families. For some, the fact that you were black and a slave meant you were family. The extended family concept is a continuation of the African perception of family, in which cousins are brothers and your friend's mother is your mother. Many African American children whose parents are absent, unavailable, or deceased have other adults and church members who—even without legal adoption—call them family and treat them as their own. "Play" aunties, mothers, and uncles are just as cherished as biological family members.

This is one of the strengths of the black community and the black church. In the twenty-first century, we must be careful to maintain the church family as a place of nurture that is ever expanding to include the least and the lost, the motherless and the fatherless. We must be careful not to bow to the gods of exclusion and partiality. It is a blessing to have a home in Christ, a spiritual or even physical place in which to fall down on one's knees and be part of the family of God.

The Last Test: Matthew 4:8-11

The devil is eager to have even Jesus bow down to him. He approaches Jesus one more time, taking him to a very high place in the cosmos where they can see all the kingdoms of the earth. No doubt they could see the kingdoms of ancient Africa and Asia. They could see the nations and the peoples from which the Mayans, Incas, and Cherokee sprang. In a pretense that he has some authority over them, the devil offers them to Jesus if only he will fall down and worship him.

How could the devil show Jesus all the kingdoms of the world and their splendor? The devil is a busy fellow. He is also a member of God's heavenly court. Job 1:6-7 states, "One day the heavenly beings came to present themselves before the LORD, and Satan [the accuser/*ha-satan*] also came among them." God asks Satan, "Where have you come from?" and Satan replies that he has been going back and forth in the earth, walking all around in it. It is part of the devil's job to know what is going on. How else can he tempt, test, and accuse us? How else can he know just how to get to us?

Jesus once again resists the devil. First, Jesus did not need anything from the devil. Neither do we. The kingdoms of the world already belong to God. "The earth is the LORD's and all that is in it" (Psalm 24:1). Second, Jesus' concern was not with gaining the kingdoms of the world but rather the kingdom of God. Jesus said that his "kingdom is not from this world" (John 18:36). Additionally, the devil offers Jesus the kingdom without the cross. For humanity, the choice between a prize versus suffering is a no-brainer. Who would want to suffer the cross when that could be avoided? The greed of society today is evidence of the insatiable desire to have the crown without the cross. Persons seeking power without "the Power" have a greater chance of yielding to temptation. If one has no relationship with God, corruption can easily set in once power and popularity are achieved. A person whose priority is on human things rather than divine things is headed for failure.

We must struggle to have righteous priorities. Peter, Jesus' star pupil, was no exception. When Jesus talks about what he must suffer, Peter selfishly requests that it be not so. Jesus pushes Peter away in disgust and even calls him Satan (Matthew 16:22-23). Jesus knows that his suffering will yield him all power and authority in heaven and on earth (Matthew 28:18), but first things first. False priorities were the foundation for the institution of slavery in America. The plantation owners wanted to become rich and powerful, and it did not matter that it took the lives of human beings to make that happen.

When we confuse our priorities, we have bowed down to Satan. When being rich and powerful is more important than fair wages and justice, we have bowed down to Satan. Our slave ancestors encourage us to bow down on our knees and pray, joining the angels of God who came to minister to Jesus upon Satan's departure. Our priority must be to worship God alone. Only those who do not trust in God put material things first. We are to "strive first for the kingdom of God and his righteousness, and all these things will be given to you as well" (Matthew 6:33).

Ponder and Wonder: Worship

The creators of "Po' Mou'ner's Got a Home at Last" remind us that it is a sad thing to have the wrong priorities. Any wrong priority is sin. We may bend our knees and bow our heads, but most importantly we must humble our spirits and bend our will to the will of God. God wants us to worship God alone (Exodus 20:1-8). Worship is the love and admiration we show for something deemed worthy. God is worthy of our praise and worship. However, God is not the only person or thing that people worship. Some worship houses and cars; others worship jobs, money, sex, or drugs. We can easily find Christians spending more time in front of the TV or Internet than in front of the Bible. Many would rather be at a sports event than in church.

We can worship God through singing, praying, sharing Communion, reading Scripture, and many other ways. We can also worship God by serving, which involves many things that we do and we do not do, such as not lying to a teacher, loving someone who is hard to love, or living a Christian lifestyle. By serving, we are glorifying God, which is worship.

We may give generously and tithe, but we must dedicate the other ninety percent to God as well. As the Lenten season continues, practice putting God first in everything that you do. Hold every area of your life up to the light of Jesus Christ. Give one hundred percent of yourself to the Lord. Do it expecting nothing but a cross.

Food for Thought

1. What is the difference between corporate worship and individual worship?
2. How do you feel when you are personally worshiping?
3. What lyrics help you understand the slaves' ideology about worship?
4. What kinds of worship styles are practiced in your church?
5. Name five characteristics of your ideal worship experience.

Closing Prayer

Gracious, dear Jesus, we love you. You are our source of peace. Teach us how to worship you in spirit and truth so that we can always find a home in your presence. Amen.

Session 4

I Couldn't Hear Nobody Pray

Luke 6:12-16

    Key Verse: Now during those days he [Jesus] went out to the mountain to pray; and he spent the night in prayer to God (Luke 6:12).

Opening Prayer: O God, you are our peace. In you we find a solace. Give us the will to keep praying and trusting that you will hear and respond. In Jesus' name. Amen.

    Spiritual: I Couldn't Hear Nobody Pray

"I Couldn't Hear Nobody Pray"

O, I couldn't hear nobody pray.
I couldn't hear nobody pray.
O, way down yonder by myself,
And I couldn't hear nobody pray.

In the mornin'.
In the noonday.
In the evenin'.

Let's Listen: A Song of Community

"I Couldn't Hear Nobody Pray" functions primarily as a communal song. It has a type of call-and-response format. *Call and response* is an African musical technique that continues to be used wherever you find black people making music. One's immediate reaction to hearing this song is to join in on the returning phrase (refrain) "couldn't hear nobody pray." The response or refrain allows the experience of the individual to become part of the experience of the community. In the recording that accompanies this study (see Leader Guide), sometimes the lead singer gives the call while the piano gives the response.

Spirituals had multiple uses. This spiritual could have been sung as the enslaved worked in the field, started up as a report by a saint of the joy experienced during a personal prayer time. The person could not hear anyone pray, for that person was alone with his or her God. Often a person would just start a song, and all those along the line would join in solidarity with the person's experience. Additionally, singing made the work more bearable. The song also could have been started up as an advance notice for a prayer meeting "way down yonder" in the hush arbor where they could not be discovered as they worshiped God, "way down yonder" where they could not be heard while praying for freedom.

The Hush Arbor: The Invisible Church

For many slaves, worship was their freedom. Many who believed held their own clandestine meetings that were invisible to the eyes of the slave masters and overseers. They held services in secret remote areas: in windowless shacks, deep in the forest, in swamps, or down by the riverside. They gathered in these places to send prayers to God and to worship. These secret places were called hush harbors, brush arbors, and/or hush arbors. Scholars call it the "invisible church" or the "invisible institution." In the hush arbor, participants could find psychic and spiritual relief from the oppression that sought to enslave not only their bodies

"Steal off slavery time in they own house and have class meeting. Driver come find 'em, whip 'em."
(Rev. Alberta Carolina, former slave in SC, 1937)

but also their minds and their spirits. Here, black folks' ways of doing worship was not wrong but truly a work of the people, incorporating African-derived patterns of speech and song. Here, the God of freedom was not captured in phrases requiring their obedience to human tyrants. Many precautions were taken to avoid being caught and heard by the masters. Severe beatings or worse resulted if their late-night prayer meetings were discovered.

The secrecy of the hush arbor was important not for deceit's sake but to protect the only sanctuary that was truly theirs. The prayer meetings served to unite the slave community under the common purpose of worship. Their worship experiences were times to renew their strength, release their tension, and fortify their hope for freedom. They believed that God would deliver them from bondage. Such things were discussed at the secret prayer meetings, and often the thought of one day obtaining freedom ignited a song or dance. They danced under the impulse of the Spirit of a new God; and they danced in ways their ancestors in Africa would have recognized. Worship was a weapon of resistance that empowered the enslaved men and women to live on.

These meetings continued even after the Civil War, as the newly freed had few resources to construct church buildings. In 1878, Bishop Daniel Payne of the African Methodist Episcopal Church (AME) exclaimed, "I attended a 'bush meeting'.... After the sermon they formed a ring, and with coats off sung, clapped their hands and stamped their feet in a most ridiculous and heathenish way."[5] It was his belief that the Negro shouts—which consisted of singing for hours, energetic body movements, thigh slapping, and foot stomping—were simply frenzy and noise. However, those who participated found spiritual engagement with God through bodily movement as well as through preaching and silent prayer.

All Night Prayer Time: Luke 6:12

Without a doubt, prayer is the greatest asset in our faith journey; and the importance of prayer takes the forefront in this Scripture lesson. Prayer is the privilege we have to communicate with God. Dialogue with God is crucial to spiritual well-being. Prayer helps to express our dependence on God. It also includes listening for the voice of God. Throughout Jesus' ministry, prayer was of supreme importance. Jesus knew that prayer was a crucial step in accomplishing his purpose.

Talking to God about our situations and circumstances helps us release our burdens and rely on God. The disciples, who would carry on after Jesus ascended, had to know how to talk to God about everything. Therefore, Jesus taught his disciples how to pray and what to say when they were praying. He gave them a model for prayer that is used to this day: the Lord's Prayer (Luke 11:2-4; Matthew 6:9-15). He was about to choose those persons who would help carry out the mission of God. The disciples would be the voice of Christianity once Jesus left. Therefore, his choice of these faithful few would impact the success of God's plan. To make such a decision, Jesus looked to the Father in prayer, and he prayed all night long.

Sometimes it is necessary to pray all night long. Enslaved Christians used prayer to help them survive. It was on the praying ground in the hush harbors that they discovered their faith and regained their hope. Whether standing, sitting, kneeling, or lying prostrate, the slaves prayed. Certainly the continuation of slavery must have left them feeling that God was silent. In such a struggle, there were sure to be times when despair was so overwhelming that no words—only groans—could be uttered. However, when we are unable to utter a word in prayer, God's Holy Spirit intercedes for us with sighs and groans too deep for words (Romans 8:26). Through it all, those praying did not forget the promise of Jesus to be with them always. Hence, their plea was "Kum ba yah, my Lord, kum ba yah. Someone's praying, Lord. Kum ba yah."

Choosing Apostles: Luke 6:13-16

After a session of prayer, Jesus was ready for his task. From the beginnings of his ministry, Jesus had called people to him to learn his teachings and discipline of love. When daytime arrived, Jesus called his disciples to him. By this passage (6:13), we know that Jesus had more than twelve disciples. The tenth chapter of Luke tells us that there were at least seventy (or seventy-two) disciples. From this number, he chose twelve to become apostles, those who would be sent to spread the gospel and to establish the church after Jesus' ascension to heaven. Among the twelve were Andrew, who brought his brother Peter to Jesus (John 1:40-42); Peter, who preached in Jerusalem, and three thousand were added to the church (Acts 2:14-41); John, the brother of James, who witnessed with Peter to the Council, and five thousand were added to the church (Acts 4:1-4); James, who was killed by King Herod for being a part of the church (Acts12:1-2); Philip, who spread the good news to Samaritans and the Ethiopian eunuch (Acts 8:4-40); and Matthew, whose Gospel story continues to spread the good news of Jesus Christ. Of course, Judas was also among the twelve, as well as the so-called "doubting" Thomas, and four others about whom we hear nothing else.

Through prayer, Jesus was able to discern who would be the best of the crowd of the disciples to lead the church. Indeed, it takes constant prayer to establish and lead churches. Through prayer, the invisible church became visible and institutional with the founding of the AUMP Church by Peter Spencer in 1813, the founding of the AME Church by Richard Allen in 1816, and the founding of the AMEZ Church in 1821 by Richard Varick. In 1815, the Richmond African Baptist Missionary Association was formed. This organization sent two missionaries to Liberia in 1821. Starting after the Civil War, black ME (now UMC) churches were established by the missionary efforts of the ME Church (North). In 1870, the CME church was also founded by the separation of black Methodists from the ME Church (South). By 1895, black Baptists all over the United States organized the National Baptist Convention as an association of churches. These accomplishments in the midst of oppression could only have happened through the prayers of the saints.[6]

Ponder and Wonder: Prayer Warriors

What is your prayer life like? Have you ever gone where nobody but Jesus could hear you pray? Today we have more preachers, praise teams, opportunities and resources for Bible studies, singing groups, evangelists, and the like. We can find a sermon just about anywhere—in books, on the television, on the Internet, on cassette tapes, on compact discs, in printed documents—you name it; it is out there. So why is there still so much evil? Within the black community, it is understood that prayer changes things. It is time for us to return to our praying roots. Prayer does not so much change the mind of God, but rather it changes us. When we pray, we are altered spiritually, emotionally, holistically, and/or intellectually. It is an honor to be asked to pray and to be known as a prayer warrior, a person who is diligent about praying for others. It is time for us to intervene through prayer on behalf of our communities and the world.

Prayer is our communication with God; it is as much listening to God as it is speaking to him. We will do well if we learn to sit in silence, listening to the voice of God through the presence of the Holy Spirit. Let us be admonished that as we listen and hear God's voice, our hearts do not harden (Hebrews 4:7). Let us heed Philippians 4:6-7: "Do not worry about anything, but in everything by prayer and supplication with thanksgiving let your requests be made known to God. And the peace of God, which surpasses all understanding, will guard your hearts and your minds in Christ Jesus." Jesus told us that we should always pray and never lose heart (Luke 18:1). During this Lenten season, let us not lose heart but rather become prayer warriors for Christ.

Food for Thought

1. How can the lyrics of this lesson's spiritual inform your prayer life?
2. In our Scripture lesson, Peter responded thinking that he knew the will of Jesus. What experience have you encountered where others felt that they knew the will of God for your life and/or the church?
3. Do you think your prayers should include world events and situations? How and why?
4. What is the role of prayer in the life of your congregation? Can this be improved?

Closing Prayer

Dear Lord, give me a praying spirit. Help me truly to mean the prayer that you taught the disciples:

Our Father, who art in heaven,
    hallowed be thy name.
    Thy kingdom come,
    thy will be done on earth as it is in heaven.
Give us this day our daily bread.
And forgive us our trespasses,
    as we forgive those who trespass against us.
And lead us not into temptation,
    but deliver us from evil.
For thine is the kingdom, and the power, and the glory, forever. Amen.

Session 5

On Ma Journey Now, Mt. Zine (Zion)

Mark 10:32-34

Key Verse: See, we are going up to Jerusalem, and the Son of Man will be handed over to the chief priests and the scribes, and they will condemn him to death; then they will hand him over to the Gentiles (Mark 10:33).

Opening Prayer: Lord God, in you we find strength to move forward. Give us the courage and determination to continue the journey. In Jesus' name. Amen.

Spiritual: On Ma Journey Now, Mt. Zine (Zion)

"On Ma Journey Now, Mt. Zine (Zion)"

Chorus:
On ma journey now, Mt. Zine,
On ma journey now, Mt. Zine.
Well, I wouldn't take nothin', Mt. Zine,
For ma journey now, Mt. Zine.

Verse 1:
One day, one day, I was walking along.
Well, the elements opened and the love came down.

Verse 2:
I went to the valley but I didn't go to stay.
Ma soul got happy an' I stayed all day.

Verse 3:
Just talk about me just as much as you please.
Well, I'll talk about you when I bend ma knees.

Let's Listen: A Song of Courage and Determination

Sung in a lively, upbeat tempo, "On Ma Journey Now, Mt. Zine" expresses a deep hope and determination of moving on, no matter the obstacles. For many blacks, as the end of the Civil War drew closer and freedom became more likely, songs about their journey to the Promised Land took on a more literal meaning. The spirituals functioned in different ways; but most importantly, they anchored the enslaved blacks to a reality that allowed them to transcend the harsh limitations of slavery. Where was Mt. Zion for the enslaved? Surely it meant a place of freedom, always for the soul and hopefully for the body.

This call-and-response "shout" was certainly acted out in the body. The rhythm lends itself to the circular shuffle of that sacred dance. The response "Mt. Zion" is more percussive and drum-like than melodic. It is a song that can "take you back" to testimony services and prayer meetings in which folk joined in and felt a part in simple, communally produced music that reached deep down into the soul.

The verses reflect personal testimony about the Christian journey. First, there is the initial experience of feeling the love of God, in which the "elements opened and the love came down." The words show how the songsters carved out a space where they could live as human beings, loved and affirmed by God. The second verse gives the testimony of a maturing Christian who goes to the valley (perhaps where nobody could hear him or her pray), not expecting much. However, the Christian has a Holy Ghost experience that lasts for hours. The lyrics of the third verse reflect a method by which the seasoned Christian handled being talked about. Whether slandered by others in the slave quarters or verbally degraded by whites, the seasoned Christian testified, "Just talk about me just as much as you please. Well, I'll talk about you when I bend ma knees."

Prayer and worship were and are key components to survival. This is a song of determination to survive whatever the conditions, a song of courage for the fearlessness it took to endure and express that they would not take anything in exchange for their journey with the Lord, even as slaves. What a miraculous attitude of perseverance! What a marvelous example for us today, a day when people kill over imagined insults and because someone has stepped on their toe. As twenty-first-century Christians, we must also model that no matter what, we will keep on the journey because God loves us, and nothing can replace a journey with God.

Mark 10:32-34: On the Way to Jerusalem

Jesus also had a journey to make, a journey through suffering and shame but ultimately to glory. Jesus is with his disciples on the way to Jerusalem. They are actually on the road "marching to Zion." Jesus is walking briskly and with purpose. The company of the disciples is lagging behind, somewhat afraid. Jesus calls the apostles (Luke 6:13-16) to come in closer. He wants to tell them something that the others may not be able to handle. He wants to tell them of his coming persecution in Jerusalem.

While those persecuted in American slavery may have viewed the mythical Mt. Zion as a place of freedom, in reality Mt. Zion for Jesus would be a place of suffering and death. In fact, on two other occasions, Jesus had already told his disciples of his pending appointment with persecution. While in Caesarea Philippi, he tells them that he will be rejected, killed, and will rise in three days. On the second occasion in Galilee, although not as detailed, Jesus says that he will be betrayed, killed, and will rise in three days. However, on the way to Jerusalem, Jesus gets specific. He explains that he will be captured, condemned to death, handed over to the Gentiles, mocked, spit on, flogged, then killed; and on the third day, he will rise. Jesus is trying to prepare the disciples for the events to come.

Jesus tells them not once but three times. This third passion prophecy details specifically the expected persecution. Common to all three predictions is Jesus' death and resurrection. The message that is crucial for the disciples to receive is that although Jesus will be killed, he will rise from the dead. Jesus' persistence in telling them about what is to come signifies his steadfast movement towards these future events. Jesus is on a journey, and nothing can deter him from what is about to happen, neither lagging and fearful disciples nor the anticipation of pain.

Persecution

The slaves no doubt empathized with Jesus upon hearing the specific details of the persecution that Jesus had to suffer. They could relate to the mocking, scourging, whipping, spitting, floggings, and killings because it occurred all around them. The hope they found in the journey now was that one day they too would rise again like Jesus. Just like the disciples were told of Jesus' persecution, the slaves were often threatened regarding their persecution. Not only were the slaves told of their persecution, they were often forced to witness it. William Wells Brown depicts a graphic scene in his novel *Clotel*. A group of slave owners pursues, captures, and later burns a slave to death for being "impudent" to his master. Four thousand slaves are brought in from neighboring plantations to witness the spectacle and to take in thoroughly what the consequences will be if they should dare to be similarly impudent. In fear of receiving the same punishment or being killed, the other slaves watch helplessly while the slave masters inflict some of the most hideous punishment known to humanity.[7]

> *"We prays for the end of Tribulation and the end of beatin's…. Some the old ones say we have to bear all, cause that all we can do…. What I hated most was when they'd beat me and I didn't know what they beat me for."* (Mary Reynolds, former slave in LA, 1937)

Jesus told his disciples about his upcoming trial because he wanted to prepare them. He wanted them to realize that the student is not greater than the teacher and that they too could expect persecution and suffering as they took up the cause of Christ. Often persons believe that when they become Christian, life will be easier, that they become entitled to material blessings, that everyone will be "nice as pie!" They demand material blessings and lose faith when their expectations are not met. They are surprised and want to retaliate when others behave in an ugly manner towards them. Many Christians resent having to suffer, even though we must participate in the suffering of Christ if we expect to participate in his glory (Romans 5:2-3).

African American slaves had no such illusion. Accepting Christianity had not been a method of relief from persecution since early colonial times. A Christian America had no mercy on a man named Dred Scott. From 1843 to 1855, Dred Scott, a slave in Missouri—supposedly a free state—petitioned the courts for his freedom and that of his family. What determination it took to submit again and again to a process that viewed him as less than human! In 1857, the U.S. Supreme Court decided that as a slave, Scott was not a U.S. citizen and had no right to petition the courts for anything. The Dred Scott decision is probably the worst ever rendered by the Supreme Court. It was overturned by the 13th and 14th amendments to the Constitution, which abolished slavery and declared all persons born or naturalized in the United States to be citizens of the United States.[8]

Ponder and Wonder: Suffering Servant

African American slaves suffered because they were black and someone—not God—had determined that being black was wrong. Isaiah 53:5 summarizes the reasons for Jesus' suffering: "He was wounded for our transgressions, / crushed for our iniquities; / upon him was the punishment that made us whole, / and by his bruises we are healed." Jesus' suffering was redemptive. He experienced it in order to redeem the souls of humankind. His punishment gives us the opportunity to be released from punishment. Without the suffering of the servant, without the shedding of his blood, there would be no forgiveness or salvation. Jesus had to shed his blood so we may have forgiveness and cleansing of sins, reconciling us to God.

"Must Jesus bear the cross alone and all the world go free? No, there's a cross for everyone, and there's a cross for me."[9] Because Dred Scott and his family suffered, the degrading, dehumanizing system of slavery was more fully exposed. Jesus bore his cross, the enslaved bore their cross, and we must bear our cross. Believers continue to be persecuted, and spiritual war never ceases. This Lenten season, let us set our face toward Jerusalem (Mt. Zine) and ready ourselves for the journey ahead so that our suffering might be redemptive, leading others into ways of peace as we follow Jesus Christ.

Food for Thought

1. Do you feel that as a Christian, you should suffer? Explain why or why not.
2. What do you think was meant in the spiritual by "the elements opened and the love came down"?
3. On your faith journey, has there been a situation where you were determined to continue in spite of adversity? Explain.

4. What methods or practices have you used to get through your time of struggle?

5. Was Jesus' suffering on the cross to show us how to get through our struggles or to show us that we would not have to struggle?

Closing Prayer

O God, you are our ever-present help in time of trouble. Give us the desire and ability to help others through their struggles. In Jesus' name. Amen.

Session 6

Were You There?

Mark 15:25-33, 37-39, 46-47

Key Verse: Truly this man was God's Son! (Mark 15:39b).

Opening Prayer: Holy God, when we cry out, grant us the grace of your hearing, your presence, and your hope. For Christ's sake. Amen.

Spiritual: Were You There?

"Were You There?"

Verse 1:
Were you there when they crucified my Lord?
Were you there when they crucified my Lord?
Oh! sometimes it causes me to tremble, tremble, tremble.
Were you there when they crucified my Lord?

Verse 2:
Were you there when they nailed him to the tree?
Were you there when they nailed him to the tree?
Oh! sometimes it causes me to tremble, tremble, tremble.
Were you there when they nailed him to the tree?

Verse 3:
Were you there when the sun refused to shine?
Were you there when the sun refused to shine?
Oh! sometimes it causes me to tremble, tremble, tremble.
Were you there when the sun refused to shine?

Let's Listen: A Song of Accountability

"Were You There?" is a familiar spiritual of few words. From verse to verse, it recites the story of Jesus' crucifixion by asking the question "Were you there?" at each step in the process. Each verse is in AA^{1}BA^2 form. The A phrases within each verse have the same words, but the melody varies. The B line acts as a refrain. It remains the same between verses, a soul-rending moan and a wrenching statement of how just the thought of the suffering makes the singer and the community feel upon seeing Jesus on the tree.

The question "Were you there?" is a statement of solidarity and a call for accountability. On one hand, it is not for literal interpretation. It expresses empathy for Christ's suffering. It asks those in the community to imagine themselves as witnesses to the event of crucifixion. At the same time, the slave creators were able to see the significance of the cross in relation to their own lives. Who had seen the horrors of slavery? And after the Civil War, who knew the identities of the white-hooded crucifiers? Where were the witnesses to their own suffering? Where, indeed, was God? They too were being crucified innocently; and for them, it was to endure the worst of the worst and keep going.

Our Christian faith is based on Christ's death, burial, and resurrection. We cannot escape the cross if we want the crown of salvation. We must accompany Jesus in this sacrifice. Listening to this spiritual as it is offered tenderly and with deep emotion, one can imagine Jesus on the cross slowly dying. Just thinking about such suffering and persecution would surely cause one to tremble. Most versions of "Were You There?" end at the tomb and are used for Good Friday service. In *Come Sunday: The Liturgy of Zion,* William B. McClain suggests a new verse that, sung joyfully, extends the spiritual to Easter morning:

"Were you there when He rose up from the dead?
Were you there when He rose up from the dead?
Oh! Sometimes I feel like shouting glory, glory, glory.
Were you there when He rose up from the dead?"[10]

During this last week of Lent, you can realize that no matter how many verses you sing, we can be excited about the victory over sin and death that we have in Jesus. Hallelujah!

Who Is "They"?

The spiritual asks, "Were you there when they…?" Perhaps we should consider the question "Who is 'they'?" Who was responsible for Jesus' appearance on a Roman cross of affliction? No doubt "they" included Judas. After all, he had a role to play. Judas was a Zealot, a member of a radical Jewish religious group that can be compared to the Black Panther Party of the 1960's and 70's. The Panthers wanted justice for black people as soon as possible, by any means possible. The first-century Zealots wanted the same for Jewish people. When Jesus proved to be non-violent, talking about a kingdom that was not of this world and not an overthrow of the Romans, Judas became disillusioned and sold out to the Sadducees.

"They" also included the Sadducees, who were the most influential and conservative of the Jewish religious groups. They ran the Jewish temple and were eager to keep the peace in Jerusalem because they had the most to lose. The Roman government allowed them to produce coinage (money) to be specifically used for temple tax. The Sadducees were like the Negroes who refused to march for Civil Rights. They might lose their job or whatever status they had in a segregated society if they let things get out of hand.

"They" also included the Pharisees, whose authority was being challenged by the teachings of Jesus. The scribes and the Pharisees were in the process of determining what it meant to be a Jew and which rabbis had it right. They were trying to figure out if Jesus was with them or against them. They were like the people who want to define what being black is. Is it determined by the way you speak, the hairstyle, the clothing, or the education? Jesus, however, was too popular. Many Pharisees joined forces with the Sadducees in stopping Jesus. Comprised of both groups, the Jewish Council used whatever clout it had with the Roman officials to get an audience with Herod and Pilate, who basically found Jesus guilty of treason. His talk of another kingdom, his influence with the people, and his talk about the first being last and the last being first sounded like a revolution. "Are you the King of the Jews?" Pilate had asked him (Mark 15:2). This man might be a threat, so "they," the Romans, crucified him.

At the Last Supper, when Jesus told the disciples around the table that someone would betray him, everyone asked, "Surely, not I?" (Mark 14:19). The answer to that question was "Yes!" Every one of them was guilty, and every one of us is also included in "they." Isaiah 53:5 reminds us that Jesus was wounded for our transgressions. It is for the sins of the world that Jesus was crucified, so the question in the spiritual could just as easily be "Were you there when we crucified our Lord?" We are there when we betray Christ with our thoughts and deeds that run counter to his teachings. We cause the Spirit of Christ to grieve daily. You and I are "they."

Mark 15:25-33, 37-39: The Crucifixion

Jesus was crucified at Golgotha, a Hebrew word meaning "the place of a skull." Crucifixion was a most cruel form of execution, reserved for criminals deemed to be a threat to the peace of the Roman Empire. It could be a thief; it could be a traitor. The hour came, and the execution took place. Over his head was the charge "The King of the Jews," a reminder of the treason of which he was accused and a warning to all who might envision some other king beside Caesar. Nevertheless, Christians know that Jesus is King of kings and Lord of lords. Jesus was crucified between two thieves, and as he hung on the tree, he was mocked. Those who passed by hurled insults, railed at him, and asked him to come down from the cross so that they would believe. Taunting Jesus, they said, "He saved others; he cannot save himself." The crowd wanted a miracle. But there was no rescue or miracle to save Jesus from the cross. Jesus was not on the cross to be saved but rather to be sacrificed for the sins of the world. In other words, for Jesus to save others, he could not save himself. By God's plan and his sacrifice, Jesus submitted himself, the Savior of the world.

After the mocking stopped, a thick darkness came over the land from noon until three in the afternoon. As the light of the Son of Man went out, the sun also refused to shine. After a loud cry, Jesus took his last breath. In the temple, the curtain that divided the Holy of Holies, or the place that separated the presence of God from the people, was torn in two. No more shall the people be separated from God. Christ is our priest. We have direct access to God through him. Surely he is the Son of God.

Mark 15:46-47: The Burial of Jesus

There was no limousine carrying Jesus' body, no family and friends riding behind the hearse, no formal service, no proclamation or resolution announced. Jesus had died just before the sabbath began, and Jewish custom forbade handling dead bodies during that period of time. The sabbath would begin at sundown. There would not be enough time to ready the body for burial. Joseph of Arimathea got permission from Pilate to take charge of Jesus' body. He was a prominent member of the Roman Council and a follower of Christ. He did minimal preparation for the body. He brought some linen cloth, took Jesus' body down, wrapped it in the linen, and placed it in a tomb; then a stone was rolled against the entrance. Mary Magdalene, Mary, and the women made note of where Jesus was laid. The women had a plan to return after the sabbath to anoint the dead body.

The Tree

While it was crucifixion for the enemies of the Roman Empire and gas chambers for the European Jews, it was the tree for blacks in America—lynching. In the years following the Civil War, the lynching of black people became an accepted method to maintain white supremacy. Racial hatred, ignorance, and fear caused mob rule, terrorism, murder, and lynching. The violence committed against Negro citizens in America by white people was simply evil. While the southern states account for 80% of lynching events—with Mississippi, Georgia, Texas, Louisiana, and Alabama leading the pack—in fact every state in the continental United States—with the exception of Massachusetts, Rhode Island, New Hampshire, and Vermont—had lynching casualties. While the victims were overwhelmingly black, whites were also included, especially Jews. Lynching often targeted blacks that were progressing economically, rising above the status that the white community believed they should hold.

> *"Some of the people I belonged to was in the Klu Klux Klan. Tolah had fo' girls and fo' boys. Some of those boys belonged. And I used to see them turn out. They went 'round whippin' n_____. They get young girls and strip 'em stark naked, and put 'em across barrels and whip 'em till the blood run out of 'em.... And ah seen it."*
> *(Richard Toler, former slave, Lynchburg, VA, 1937)*

Resisting most certainly meant increased violence. Nevertheless, the pioneer crusader against lynching was a black woman named Ida B. Wells Barnett. As editor of the Memphis *Free Speech,* she rallied anti-lynching sentiment in the United States and England and published several pamphlets exposing the barbarity of lynching, including *A Red Record,* written in 1895.[11] "In 1900, Negro Congressman George White introduced America's first anti-lynching bill, only to see it die in the House Judiciary Committee."[12] From 1909, the NAACP campaigned vigorously against lynching and all forms of racism and discrimination. By 1922, the NAACP's attempts to secure federal anti-lynching legislation, such as the Dyer Anti-Lynching Bill, were unsuccessful.[13]

The hanging of black men and women upon trees after mutilation and torture was so frequent that in the late 1930's Lewis Allan wrote a song about it, "Strange Fruit," sung and recorded by Billie Holiday.[14] The song describes the strange fruit born by southern trees, black bodies swinging in the wind, with eyes bulging out and mouths twisted around. These trees had bloody roots and blood-spattered leaves. And around them, the magnolia scents mingled with the smell of burning flesh. So apt is this description that even one who has never seen a lynching can picture it in his or her mind. You can hear the families of the lynched singing "Were You There?" as they cut down their loved ones from the tree. The song asks for accountability even as all-white juries let the guilty go free and the federal government turned its head.

Ponder and Wonder: Repentance

On June 14, 2005, the U.S. Senate finally offered an apology for historically failing to back anti-lynching legislation that would have given some justice and relief to the black community many years ago. As Bishop Desmond Tutu has shown the world, the healing can only begin with the telling of the truth. He conducted the Truth and Reconciliation hearings of South Africa (1995–98) in order to promote healing from apartheid. Perpetrators of violence had to face those families that had been victimized by the terror and sometimes received the mercy they had not shown. Telling the truth is part of repentance, and it is never too late to repent. God waits with open arms to hear our confessions and grant forgiveness. We too must be willing to confess our sins to one another and seek healing.

"Anyone hung on a tree is under God's curse" (Deuteronomy 21:23b). The strange fruit of American trees had good company, for Jesus was also hung on a tree. He "made his grave with the wicked" (Isaiah 53:9a) and "was numbered with the transgressors" (53:12b). Jesus' act of sacrificial love was offered as an apology for the sins of the world. His trial on the cross even redeemed the meaning of the cross. The old rugged cross—rather than a symbol of suffering and shame—is one of healing, love, and beauty. As the season of Lent comes to a close, we must be truthful and confess our sins, allowing the beauty of Jesus' sacrifice to heal our spirit as we love one another. Repent, for the kingdom of God is near!

Food for Thought

1. After hearing the spiritual, what are your thoughts regarding the suffering of Jesus? Of black Americans?
2. How do we know that we are part of the "they" who crucified Jesus?
3. Crucifixion was a form of capital punishment or death sentence. What are your thoughts on capital punishment?
4. What role did the various religious groups in Judea play in the conviction and death of Jesus?
5. What are ways to promote healing in our world?
6. Write an apology for your sins, perhaps to God or to someone else you have wronged.

Closing Prayer

Dear God, thank you for your grace and mercy. Empower us to be gracious and merciful to others. Thank you for showing us such love. Enable us to be channels of the love of Jesus Christ in this world. In Jesus' name we pray. Amen.

Endnotes

Session 1 – This Lonesome Valley

1. From *The Spirituals and the Blues*, by James H. Cone (Orbis Books, 1972, 1991); pages 60–61.
2. See *African Americans: Voices of Triumph – Perseverance*, by the editors of Time-Life Books (Time-Life Books, 1993); pages 42–47. See *Africans in America: America's Journey Through Slavery*, Parts 1, 2, 3, 4; http://www.pbs.org/wgbh/aia/. See http://www.juneteenth.com/middlep.htm.

Session 2 – A City Called Heaven

3. See *African Americans: Voices of Triumph – Perseverance*; page 29. See *Africans in America: America's Journey Through Slavery*, Parts 1, 2, 3, 4; http://www.pbs.org/wgbh/aia/. See *The Trouble I've Seen: The Big Book of Negro Spirituals*, by Bruno Chenu (Judson Press, 2003); page 7.
4. From *Narrative of the Life of Frederick Douglass, an American Slave*, by Frederick Douglass (Anti-Slavery Office, 1845); page 188 (appendix of book); http://docsouth.unc.edu/douglass/douglass.html.

Session 4 – I Couldn't Hear Nobody Pray

5. From *Recollections of Seventy Years*, by Bishop Daniel Alexander Payne and Reverend C.S. Smith (Publishing House of the A.M.E. Sunday School Union, 1888); page 253; http://docsouth.unc.edu/church/payne70/payne.html.
6. See *The Chronological History of the Negro in America*, by Peter M. Bergman and Mort N. Bergman (Mentor Books, 1969); pages 105, 116, 266, 315. See the following Web sites: http://www.c-m-e.org/; http://docsouth.unc.edu/church/payne70/payne.html; and http://docsouth.unc.edu/church/fisher/fisher.html. For more information, see *The Trouble I've Seen*; pages 62–66. Also see *Africans in America: America's Journey Through Slavery*, Parts 1, 2, 3, 4; http://www.pbs.org/wgbh/aia/.

Session 5 – On Ma Journey Now, Mt. Zine (Zion)

7. See *Clotel, or, The President's Daughter,* by William Wells Brown (Penguin Books, 2004). The first novel published by an African American, *Clotel* takes up the story, in circulation at the time, that Thomas Jefferson fathered an illegitimate mulatto daughter who was sold into slavery. William Well Brown, though born into slavery, escaped to become one of the most prominent reformers of the nineteenth century and one of the earliest historians of the black experience. The original 1853 edition is available as free e-text from Project Gutenberg: http://gutenberg.net/etext/2046.

8. See *African Americans: Voices of Triumph – Perseverance*; page 39. You may also do a search for "Dred Scott" at The U.S. National Archives and Records Administration: http://www.archives.gov.

9. From *The United Methodist Hymnal*, No. 424 (The United Methodist Publishing House, 1989); words: Thomas Shepherd and others, 1855; music: George N. Allen, 1844

Session 6 – Were You There?

10. From *Come Sunday: The Liturgy of Zion,* by William B. McClain (Abingdon Press, 1990); page 107.

11. See *The African American Century: How Black Americans Shaped Our Country*, by Henry Louis Gates Jr. and Cornel West (The Free Press, 2000); pages 35–38.

12. From *The Negro Holocaust: Lynching and Race Riots in the United States, 1880–1950,* by Robert A. Gibson (Yale-New Haven Teachers Institute, 1978–2005); http://www.yale.edu/ynhti/curriculum/units/1979/2/79.02.04.x.html.

13. See *The Chronological History of the Negro in America*; pages 357–59, 402–03.

14. See *The African American Century: How Black Americans Shaped Our Country*; pages 164–68.